Geysers

Other books in the Wonders of the World series include:

Gems
Icebergs
Mummies
Quicksand

WONDERS
OF THE **WORLD**

Geysers

P.M. Boekhoff and Stuart A. Kallen

KIDHAVEN
PRESS™

THOMSON
™
GALE

San Diego • Detroit • New York • San Francisco • Cleveland
New Haven, Conn. • Waterville, Maine • London • Munich

© 2003 by KidHaven Press. KidHaven Press is an imprint of The Gale Group, Inc., a division of Thomson Learning, Inc.

KidHaven™ and Thomson Learning™ are trademarks used herein under license.

For more information, contact
KidHaven Press
27500 Drake Rd.
Farmington Hills, MI 48331-3535
Or you can visit our Internet site at http://www.gale.com

LIBRARY OF CONGRESS CATALOGING-IN-PUBLICATION DATA

Boekhoff, P.M. (Patti Marlene), 1957–
   Geysers / by P.M. Boekhoff and Stuart A. Kallen.
      p. cm. — (Wonders of the world)
Summary: Discusses what geysers are, where they are located, why they erupt, how different kinds of geysers behave, and their interactions with their environments.
Includes bibliographical references (p.).
   ISBN 0-7377-1029-2 (hardback : alk. paper)
    1. Geysers—Juvenile literature. [1. Geysers.] I. Kallen, Stuart A., 1955– II. Title.
   GB1198.5 B64 2003
   551.2'3—dc21

2002001269

Printed in the United States of America

CONTENTS

How Geysers Are Made

A geyser is a hot spring that sometimes shoots very hot water and steam into the air. Geysers are born in hot springs, pools of water that flow from lakes deep within the earth. Yellowstone Park in Wyoming has thousands of hot springs. More than four hundred of these springs are geysers. This is more than all the geysers in the rest of the world combined.

The geysers in Yellowstone and other places often form in groups, called geyser fields. The second-largest geyser field in the United States is at Umnak Island, just off the coast of Alaska. The remote island has twelve geysers.

Geysers Around the World

Geysers are found in parts of the world where volcanoes have shaped the landscape. The island of Iceland was formed

Yellowstone's most famous geyser, Old Faithful, spews a tall column of steam.

by more than one hundred volcanoes, and it is full of geysers. In the year 1294 a large earthquake awakened many geysers there, and they became famous in Europe. Soon, all geysers became known by the Icelandic name *geysir* (or geyser), which means "gusher" in the Icelandic language.

Another two hundred geysers spray and gurgle in the Valley of Geysers in Kamchatka, Russia. And about sixty-seven small geysers erupt at various times in El Tatio, in the Andes Mountains in Chile—an area surrounded by active volcanoes.

The Earth's Crust

To find out what makes a geyser form, scientists look at the layers of materials that make up the earth. The earth's outer layer, called the crust, is made up of volcanic soil, sand, and dirt. The earth's crust is very thin compared to the layer just below the crust, called the mantle. The mantle is made of **magma**, a volcanic rock that is so hot (up to 7,500°F), that it has melted into a thick liquid paste.

Where the earth's crust is especially thin, as it is in geyser fields such as Yellowstone, it is easily broken. The thin crust of dirt moves slowly over the hot magma, creating a path of craters and volcanoes over the centuries. Yellowstone Park sits atop a huge old volcano that erupted and collapsed, creating a deep valley partly filled with lava. This type of valley is known as a **caldera**.

The Hot Spot

Three miles below the surface of the Yellowstone valley, or caldera, is a hot spot in the mantle, called the mantle

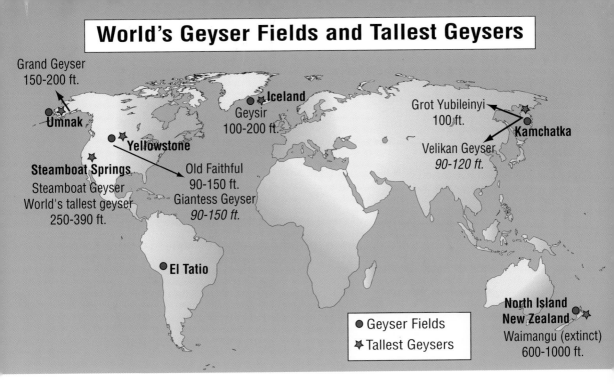

World's Geyser Fields and Tallest Geysers

Grand Geyser
150-200 ft.

Umnak

Iceland
Geysir
100-200 ft.

Grot Yubileinyi
100 ft.

Kamchatka

Velikan Geyser
90-120 ft.

Yellowstone

Steamboat Springs
Steamboat Geyser
World's tallest geyser
250-390 ft.

Old Faithful
90-150 ft.
Giantess Geyser
90-150 ft.

El Tatio

North Island
New Zealand
Waimangu (extinct)
600-1000 ft.

● Geyser Fields
✹ Tallest Geysers

plume, about twelve miles across. The mantle plume brings the super hot magma close to the surface of the earth. As the magma boils and churns below, the hot spot wells up and puts stress on the thin crust of the caldera.

More than 300 million years ago, shallow seas filled the Yellowstone caldera. Under the seas, magma boiled and bubbled, breaking through the thin, stressed crust and mixing with seawater. Giant bubbles in the hot magma became underground caves filled with steamy seawater and volcanic gases. Within these ancient caves the underground plumbing system of a hot spring or geyser is formed.

Geyser Plumbing Systems

Hot geysers shoot out of underground caves through naturally formed underground tubes that act like garden hoses spraying water into the air. These plumbing systems depend on **minerals**, gases, and even microscopic living creatures to form.

The water in the underground caves is rich with minerals such as sulfur and iron that seep out of the earth. Volcanic gas, called carbon dioxide, (the same gas that gives soda pop its fizz) makes the boiling mineral water dance with bubbles in the underground cave. Amazingly, tiny little one-celled creatures are able to survive in the scalding hot water of the underground caves. When they die, their shells settle out of the water, along with sulfur or iron. These tiny bits of material are cemented together to form solid crystal minerals that create a hard stony lining along the **faults** and the cave walls in the plumbing systems of geysers.

The most common geyser-forming crystal mineral in Yellowstone Park is called geyserite. This material collects along the plumbing system and seals it like a milky white glass bottle. It lines the underground caves as well as the paths that lead up to the surface of the earth. If there were no geyserite to seal up the cracks in the plumbing, the water would leak out of the caves into the earth. Then the geysers could not erupt because they would not have a sealed path directing the water to the earth's surface.

The Geyser Erupts

Geysers erupt because of the pressure and heat that build up in the underground caves. This happens when the weight of the earth above presses down on the water in the caves below. The pressure keeps the water from erupting into a boil as the magma wells up and makes the water hotter and hotter. (Water usually boils at 212°F.)

Sometimes the geyser water reaches 500°F or more before it finally erupts into a boil and releases steam, which expands very quickly. This creates even more pressure in the plumbing system. The steam is forced out, pushing some of the water through the fault to the surface of the earth above.

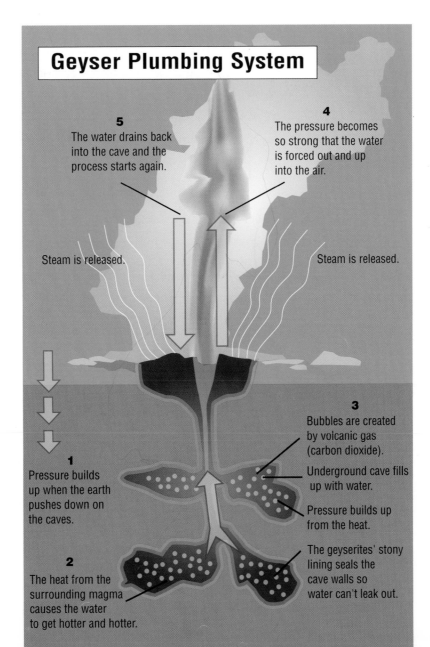

Geyser Plumbing System

5 The water drains back into the cave and the process starts again.

4 The pressure becomes so strong that the water is forced out and up into the air.

Steam is released.

Steam is released.

3 Bubbles are created by volcanic gas (carbon dioxide).

Underground cave fills up with water.

Pressure builds up from the heat.

1 Pressure builds up when the earth pushes down on the caves.

The geyserites' stony lining seals the cave walls so water can't leak out.

2 The heat from the surrounding magma causes the water to get hotter and hotter.

A bright rainbow appears in the steam from a geyser in Yellowstone.

The steam hisses and spits, then the water gushes out. When it bubbles to the surface, the stresses in the earth's crust are relieved and the water is cooled by the air. After it gushes out, the water drains back down into the underground cave to be heated again.

Lives of a Geyser

Sometimes a geyser will stop erupting, and the geyserite will form into soil. Trees may grow in the soil, then die from the hot water when the geyser starts up again. Geyserite then gathers on the logs, making them look like beautiful stones, called wood opal or petrified wood. Scientists can study this petrified wood to tell how long a geyser has existed.

These studies have shown that Yellowstone's Old Faithful, for instance, became active as a hot spring about 750 years ago. After 450 years as a hot spring, Old Faithful became a geyser about 300 years ago. But Old Faithful sits on top of much older geyserite, which formed an earlier

Geysers are found where volcanoes once helped shape the landscape.

spring. No one knows how long Old Faithful has been changing and growing.

In 1992 scientists sent a video camera down the geyserite pipe of Old Faithful. Forty-five feet under the ground, the camera saw a cave the size of a large car filled with actively boiling water.

There are still many mysteries to be discovered about geysers. These great natural wonders have a life of their own, and much of it takes place deep under the earth.

CHAPTER
TWO

Geysers on Land

Although geysers may be located some distance from each other on the earth's surface, they are often connected to each other underground. Because geysers in a geyser field are often connected, when one erupts it has an effect on all the others that are attached to it.

When one geyser erupts, it changes the amount of heat and water flowing into geysers connected to it. No one knows how far these connections go, though it has been shown that geysers at least twenty-five miles away from each other may be connected underground. This is one of the reasons geyser eruptions can be unpredictable.

Geyser fields are always changing. For instance, Steamboat Geyser in Yellowstone stopped erupting for a while after an earthquake. Instead, Monarch Geyser, one

A cone geyser in Yellowstone erupts, sending steam high into the air.

of its neighbors that had been sleeping for eighty-one years, began to erupt.

Cone Geysers

Cone geysers have round cones like a volcano. The cones are formed by drops of water that continuously spray from the geyser between major eruptions. The spray contains geyserite and other minerals. When the mineral water sprays out, it is cooled by the air and the minerals turn into tiny little crystals that form platforms, terraces, and cones on the surface. Some of this spray contains minerals that color the geyserite. For example, Pink Cone Geyser, located in Yellowstone, has a pink geyserite cone because its spray contains the mineral manganese dioxide.

Cone geysers are usually the most predictable kind of geysers because they usually have only one underground cave as a water source. Old Faithful is a predictable cone geyser whose eruptions are between forty-five minutes and two hours apart, and shoot up to 180 feet in the air. It has this regular schedule because all of its water erupts out of one cave.

Because of their dramatic eruptions, cone geysers are the largest and most well-known type of geyser in the world. For example, Steamboat Geyser in Yellowstone is the tallest active geyser in the world. Once in a great while, every five to fifty years, it shoots a column of steaming hot mineral water three hundred feet into the air. After three to thirty minutes of such a major eruption, it roars and thunders and steams for hours. Steamboat's opening, called a vent, is caked with minerals. This creates a nozzle that helps the cone geyser shoot a forceful column of water high into the air.

Fountain Geysers

Most geysers do not erupt faithfully because their plumbing is not simple. They may have two or more underground lakes connected by their plumbing system, which are connected together. These geysers usually form fountains that erupt much less regularly than cone geysers.

Fountain geysers are the most common type of geyser. They look like fountains, with water bubbling up into a surface crater that fills to the rim with water before an eruption. Rising steam shoots through the pool of water, bubbling, splashing, and spraying little jets that play along the surface of the water in the crater. This is called preplay, and is often a sign that the fountain geyser is getting ready to erupt.

As more steam forms under the fountain, it pushes more water up until it erupts through the water in the fountain. The water sprays up to twenty-five feet in the air. When the eruption is over, some of the water in the crater drains back down into the plumbing system. Slowly, water refills the plumbing system and the cycle starts again. Some geysers refill in minutes, while others may take months to recover.

Bead Geyser in Yellowstone is a fountain geyser. It was named for the loose round balls of geyserite, called beads and eggs, that were once found around the geyser. These objects are formed in the splashing fountain, which keeps them moving so they do not stick to the surface. The geyser eggs and beads at Bead Geyser were so beautiful that they were picked up by tourists long ago. But the crater that holds Bead Geyser's fountain is still lined with lovely, delicate beadlike shapes.

Fumaroles

A geyser's eruption will stop suddenly when it runs out of heat. But there is usually enough water saved up in the plumbing system for the next eruption. However, some geysers have more heat than water. These geysers erupt first with water, followed by an eruption of steam.

When the water in the plumbing system is very low, a geyser may spout only steam. These geysers are known as

A gigantic plume of water and steam spouts from the Geysir in Iceland.

A fumarole, or steam vent, forms along Fountain Paint Pot Trail in Yellowstone.

fumaroles, or steam vents, and they are simply giant smoking holes in the ground. Fumaroles are the hottest kind of hot spring. They are so hot, in fact, that all the water boils away and turns to steam before it reaches the surface.

Although most geysers form in basins where there is plenty of water, fumaroles often form on the sides of volcanoes where it is drier. Yellowstone's Fountain Paint Pot Trail, for example, includes some fumaroles that have formed in the higher, drier regions of the park.

Small amounts of gasses, such as carbon dioxide or hydrogen sulfide, may also come out with the steam. (Hydrogen sulfide contains sulfur, which smells like rotten eggs.) When the sulfur vapor meets the cool moist air above the fumarole, it crystallizes around the opening, making beautiful yellow sulfur crystals.

Mud Pots

If the crater around the vent of a fumarole is filled with hot water, little creatures in the water eat the hydrogen out of hydrogen sulfide, releasing a chemical called sulfuric acid.

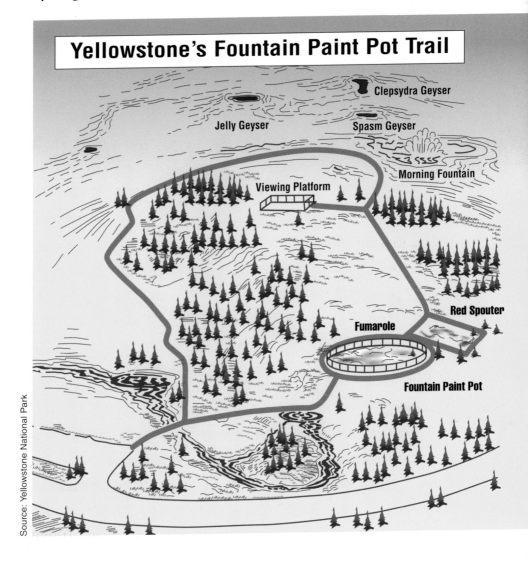

Yellowstone's Fountain Paint Pot Trail

Clepsydra Geyser

Jelly Geyser

Spasm Geyser

Morning Fountain

Viewing Platform

Red Spouter

Fumarole

Fountain Paint Pot

Source: Yellowstone National Park

This strong acid dissolves nearby rocks into a thick layer of wet clay. This creates what is known as a mud pot.

Under the mud pot, volcanic gases and water combine to make steam. When the steam rises to the surface of the mud pot, the mud in the crater sputters and plops like thick soup boiling on a stove. Sometimes these scalding hot acidic bubbles can gurgle out of the ground, threatening plants and wildlife nearby. For example, the Astringent Creek mud pot in Yellowstone once hurled huge blobs of mud almost one hundred feet into the air, killing nearby trees.

Hot acidic bubbles sputter out of a mud pot.

When rain and melting snow supply more water in the mud pot, the mud becomes thin, and spits and bubbles. In the dry seasons the mud becomes thicker, and the steam hisses, wheezes, and sighs as it puffs its way up through the chunky mud. These bubbles can become very large before they loudly burst. For example, when the huge clay bubbles of Yellowstone's Mud Volcano break, people can hear them pop more than a mile away.

Sometimes the drying mud becomes as thick as cement, piling up around the vent, creating a cone-shaped mound of mud. Inside, bubbles of boiling mud burst open, thumping on the sides of the cone. If the vent gets clogged with mud, pressure builds up until it erupts as a mud volcano, spewing mud in every direction. At the Mushpots mud pots in Yellowstone, one giant mud pot hurled chunks of mud as big as a cabin. If the mud dries up completely, however, and the vent stays open, the mud pot may turn into a fumarole.

When the natural white clay in a mud pot is colored by minerals, it is called a paint pot. Yellows come mostly from sulfur. Oranges, pinks, reds, browns, and blacks come from iron oxides and iron sulfides.

A Changing Landscape

Some formations, such as Red Spouter in Yellowstone, act like geysers, fumaroles, and mud pots depending on the season. During summer, when the water is low, Red Spouter is a fumarole. From late fall through the winter, water forms around its vent, and it spouts red water and mud. When the water level is high in spring, it forms a runny red paint pot.

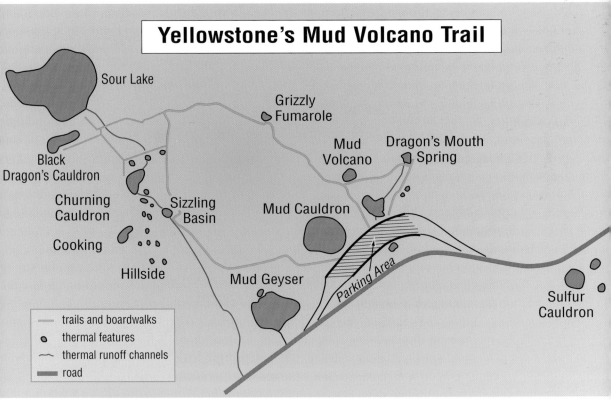

Yellowstone's Mud Volcano Trail

Sour Lake

Grizzly
Fumarole

Black
Dragon's Cauldron

Mud
Volcano

Dragon's Mouth
Spring

Churning
Cauldron

Sizzling
Basin

Mud Cauldron

Cooking

Hillside

Mud Geyser

Parking Area

Sulfur
Cauldron

— trails and boardwalks
○ thermal features
⌒ thermal runoff channels
▬ road

Source: Yellowstone National Park

From a steaming, sputtering fumarole to a giant
gusher, geysers come in many shapes and sizes. The way a
geyser acts depends upon the amount of heat and water
that feeds it. Geysers in Yellowstone spout water from a
basin that once held an ancient sea. Now there is no sea in
the Yellowstone basin, but geysers still gush from underground lakes deep within the earth.

Geysers in the Ocean

T housands of geysers exist under the ocean, but instead of shooting hot water and minerals into the air, they gush into the cold ocean waters. Scientists who study oceans, called oceanographers, have found many geysers in a long line of underwater volcanoes that circle the earth, called the Mid-Ocean Ridge. Oceanographers use specially designed research vehicles to study these extreme places, in an environment where no human could otherwise survive.

Underwater geysers are called hydrothermal vents. (Hydro means water and thermal means heat.) These vents usually form together in fields, just like the geysers on land.

Black Smokers

In the valley between volcanoes on the Mid-Ocean Ridge, the ocean floor stretches apart and cracks open. Cold seawater seeps down into the cracks and sinks down several miles, where it is heated by the magma below. The tremendous weight of the sea puts pressure on the hot water. Like geysers on land, when the water is under great pressure, it does not boil until it gets extremely hot.

Enriched with minerals from magma, the superheated water rises back up to the seafloor and gushes into the ocean. The vent water may be as hot as 750°F when it gushes out. But it cools quickly, and within an inch of the vent opening, the temperature is the same as most deep seawater, which may be only 34°F, a few degrees above freezing.

Hot liquefied minerals, such as sulfur, iron, copper, mercury, gold, lead, silver, tin, arsenic, uranium, cadmium, and zinc, turn solid in the cold ocean water. They form clouds of crystal minerals that look like black smoke. For this reason these geysers are called black smokers.

Chimneys

After these minerals solidify, they fall to the ocean floor and pile up in formations around the hot vents. Over time the minerals build up to form cones that look like chimneys. Different minerals form crystals of different colors. Chimneys may be brown, green, white, or orange. Some are tall and thin like steeples; others have onion-shaped domes on top. They may have shelflike overhangs that trap hot water rising from below, creating upside-down shimmering hot pools.

Black smokers form much more quickly than cone geysers form on land. On land a geyser cone grows about

Twin black smokers vent on the ocean floor.

one inch every hundred years. A black smoker cone may grow twenty feet in just one year. If they are not broken up or destroyed, black smokers may grow as large as the formation known as Godzilla, a black smoker in the Pacific Ocean off the coast of Oregon. This amazing natural creation was once as tall as a fifteen-story building—about 150 feet high.

White Smokers

About ten miles away from the Mid-Ocean Ridge is an undersea mountain range with a giant mountain called Atlantis Massif. It rises twelve thousand feet from the ocean floor, and if it were on land it would be about the same size as Mount Rainier in Washington. Atlantis Massif was formed by an earthquake fault that lifted up ancient deep volcanic lava rock from several miles under the seafloor to more than two miles above the seafloor. And this rock is made from a glassy green mineral called olivine or peridotite.

Along the slopes of the Atlantis Massif are geysers called white smokers, which release minerals that turn white. This is caused by calcium, the most abundant material in the smoker. Small amounts of other white minerals such as barium and silicon are also included. The seawater in these geysers is heated and mixed with minerals under the seafloor, but the water it releases is between about 100°F and 150°F, much cooler than the water released by a black smoker.

When the white mineral water rises through faults, it mixes with the peridotite in the mountain. This causes the

Peridotite makes up the Atlantis Massif.

glassy green mineral to change into a dull green jadelike mineral called serpentine. When the white mineral water flows out into the cold sea, it crystallizes into white limestone ledges and stalagmites that form white spiraling towers and chimneys. The highest spiral on the Atlantis Massif is 180 feet tall. Scientists have named this formation Poseidon after the ancient Greek god of the sea. Steep-sided mounds, chimneys, and spiraling towers of gleaming white rock blossom into feathery ledges thirty feet wide.

Hundreds of overlapping ledges form down the slope of Atlantis Massif, like the hot spring fountains in Yellowstone National Park. Trapped under the ledges, warm pools support dense mats of bacteria that shimmer in the

Stalagmites similar to these cave formations spiral upward around Atlantis Massif.

rising vent water. They are similar to the ancient sea creatures that form geyserite in the geysers on land.

Shallow Underwater Geysers

The top of Atlantis Massif is less than a half mile below the ocean's surface and is covered with shallow-water seashells. It is flat and weathered, and oceanographers believe it may have once been an island rising above the sea. The white smokers along its slopes, like those surrounding Iceland, are formed in shallow waters.

Iceland is located on a formation called the Iceland Plateau, formed from large volcanoes that rise out of the sea along the Mid-Atlantic Ridge. Many small islands rise out of the sea around the big island. For many years, fishermen noticed steam and gas bubbles rising out of white smokers in the shallow water near these small islands.

These geysers are similar to geysers on land, except that they have an unlimited supply of water. Boiling water and great violent blasts of steam often erupt from these shallow underwater geysers.

An Icelandic ocean geyser shoots steam into the sky.

A geyser's blast sends water and steam hundreds of feet into the air.

In this area black smokers also throw mud and minerals out of the sea and into the air. Earthquakes rock the islands, and volcanoes explode out of the water to form new land. Under the sea or on the land, the geysers that form near these volcanoes are living wonders. They are mysterious and beautiful and they hold awesome power to shape the entire planet. Where there are geysers, life is abundant and full of surprises.

CHAPTER FOUR

Geyser Life

Although the water of geysers is extremely hot, the rich mineral soup that gushes out of geysers supports a wide variety of lush plants and exotic animals. Although most life is scattered thinly through the ocean, the geyser environment is packed with amazing creatures of all kinds. Thousands of these odd, tiny life-forms make geysers as rich in diversity as rain forests.

Animals that look like undersea flowers are nibbled on by fish with plantlike forms growing out of their bodies. Over the years, more than three hundred exciting new kinds of life have been discovered living around geysers. Some of these life-forms do not exist anywhere else on Earth. Each geyser field is a unique environment, with different kinds of life-forms.

Archaea

When new geysers are formed under the sea, the first life-forms settle like falling snow around the vents. They grow together to form white mats several inches thick, growing tendrils to attach themselves to the ocean floor. Some scientists believe these tiny creatures may be the oldest forms of life on Earth, so they named them **archaea**, or ancient ones.

These ancient, heat-loving creatures form the basis of lush **ecosystems** on the edges of volcanoes and hot springs, including geysers on land and in the sea. They have been found living in an even hotter area beneath the ocean's floor, and scientists believe they rise from below when the vent is ready to come to life. They also come up from the hot rocks under geysers on land. They live up to two and a half miles under the surface of the earth, where the magma meets the water.

Microscopic archaea dwell on the edge of a geyser's vent.

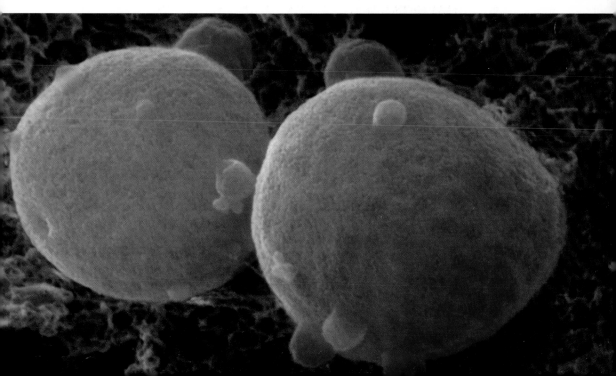

Unlike life on dry land, sunlight is not the main source of energy for archaea. They begin their lives in deep darkness, creating life energy from minerals that gush out of geysers, such as hydrogen, sulfur, and methane. In turn, all the other creatures that live around the geysers depend upon the archaea for their food.

The Octopus's Garden

Around black smokers millions of tiny archaea live inside larger life-forms that look like combinations between worms and plants. There are many kinds of these amazing plantlike worms that form at the vents, but the largest is called the tube worm. Dark red plumes on their heads grow out of a white tube, making them look like giant tubes of red lipstick twelve feet long. If they are disturbed, they can pull their red plume heads down into the tube.

The plumes are filled with blood, which gives life and breath to the white archaea that live inside the tube. Ghostly white crabs and white snakelike eelpout fish with bulging eyes nibble off the red plumes. Giant chalky white clams reach a long, bright red foot down into the sulfur-rich vent water. Tiny snail-like animals, sea anemones, sea stars, translucent fish, weird scary looking fish, mussels, tiny lobsters, skates, big and little squid, and even octopuses feed at some vents.

The octopus is very shy, as are many of the creatures who live near the vents. At the bottom of the cold, dark sea, a mysterious pale light flows from the vents. It shimmers so softly it is impossible to see with the human eye. The spotlights scientists use to study the vents are so

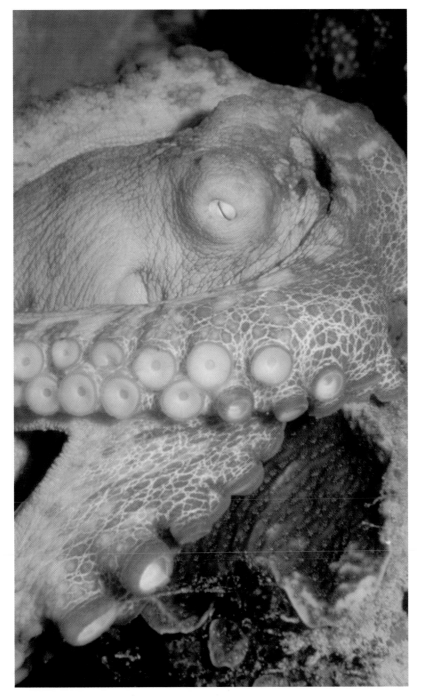

An octopus feeds on archaea at the vents of an under-water geyser.

A startled researcher runs from an erupting geyser.

bright that they believe the lights destroyed the eyesight of some of these shy creatures just by looking at them.

Studying the Vents

The discovery of such sensitive, wonderful ecosystems long hidden in the deep darkness around hydrothermal vents has caused scientists to examine ways to protect and explore at the same time. Because each vent seems to be a unique ecosystem with unique life-forms, scientists are now aware that unless they are careful, whole communities could be destroyed.

Scientists believe it is important to continue studying geysers because of what they reveal about life on Earth. White smokers, for example, create an environment similar to conditions on Earth more than 3 billion years ago, when it is believed that living creatures first emerged. Researchers believe that the archaea that rise out of the cooler water of these white smokers may represent the earliest form of life on Earth.

There are millions of kinds of archaea and other creatures around the vents. The life-forms that are present at the vents differ between vent sites and between oceans. For example, shrimp and sea anemones are found mostly in the Atlantic, and tube worms and clams live mostly in the Pacific. Archaea are the basic life-forms that support rich, lush ecosystems in all kinds of geysers.

Colorful Water Creatures

Without archaea there might be no geysers. On land archaea fossils form white geyserite to hold the ancient seawater in underground caves. Archaea fossils form the cones that allow geysers to gush high into the air, as well as the fountains that catch it. And the geyserite plumbing carefully channels the ancient seawater back into the earth, where it is warmed again.

This action brings up minerals from below that provide food for many of the microscopic plants and animals that live in the geysers. All kinds of tiny, ancient creatures color the geyser water different colors. Because each species can survive only in certain temperatures, it is often possible to tell how hot a geyser is by the color of its pool.

A hot spring in New Zealand, called Champagne, is pink from the bacteria that live in very hot water, above 180°F. The coolest geyser water (between 122°F and 164°F) is colored by yellow, orange, red, and green algae.

Life Springs

The bacteria and algae in geysers in turn provide food for an entire web of life. Ephydrid flies, for example, feed on the microscopic creatures. The flies in turn provide the only food for wolf spiders. The spiders are eaten by kill-deers, birds that live around geyser basins. Trumpeter swans and trout also make their home in the channels carrying geyser water, and these provide food for the bears who live in the park.

A family of grizzly bears plays in a channel fed by geyser water.

Three cone geysers spray in unison.

Aboveground and under the ocean, geysers are some of the most sensitive, fragile environments on the planet. But they are also some of the most diverse and exciting places to explore.

Glossary

archaea: Ancient ones; a unique form of life discovered in geysers.

caldera: A large crater formed by the collapse of a volcano.

ecosystem: Communities of living things in their environment.

faults: Breaks in the rocks in the earth's crust, caused by shifting and shaking by earthquakes, meteors, and other events.

fumarole: A hot spring low in water, which gives out fumes.

magma: Hot liquid rock under the earth's crust, which forms lava and volcanoes on the surface of the earth.

minerals: Hard, crystal-shaped natural materials found in the ground or in water, including sand, iron, sulfur, salt, coal, stone, and gems.

For Further Exploration

Patricia Armentrout, *Hot Springs and Geysers.* Vero Beach, FL: Rourke Press, 1996. Discusses the different kinds of hot springs, including geysers.

Larry Dane Brimner, *Geysers: A True Book.* New York: Childrens Press, 2000. Describes what geysers are, where they are found, and how they are formed.

T. Scott Bryan, *Geysers: What They Are and How They Work.* Niwot, CO: Robert Rhinehart, 1990. Explores geysers, how they are related to each other and to other kinds of hot springs, and how they change over time.

Roy A. Gallant, *Geysers: When Earth Roars.* New York: Franklin Watts, 1997. Discusses how geysers are formed, where they are, how they are used by humans, and their extinction.

Alice Gilbreath, *Nature's Squirt Guns, Bubble Pipes, and Fireworks: Geysers, Hot Springs, and Volcanoes.* Drawings by Jo Polseno; describes how geysers work by comparing them to a squirt gun, and compares hot springs to bubble pipes.

Index